12/06

DATE DUE

JAN 1 7 2007	
MAR 1 5 2007	
MAR 2 6 2007	
APR 1 3 2007	
MAY 1 2 2007	

DEMCO, INC. 38-2931

OWEN & MZEE

THE TRUE STORY OF A REMARKABLE FRIENDSHIP

Told by ISABELLA HATKOFF, CRAIG HATKOFF, and DR. PAULA KAHUMBU

With photographs by PETER GRESTE

SCHOLASTIC PRESS / NEW YORK

THIS BOOK IS DEDICATED TO THE MEMORY OF THE NEARLY 250 EMPLOYEES OF THE LAFARGE GROUP WHO PERISHED OR WHO ARE STILL MISSING FROM THE TSUNAMI THAT OCCURRED ON DECEMBER 26, 2004. YOU MAY VISIT WWW.LAFARGEECOSYSTEMS.COM TO FIND OUT HOW TO HELP THEIR FAMILIES.

PRONUNCIATION GUIDE

Aldabra	al-DAH-brah
Malindi	mah-LIN-dee
Mombasa	mom-BAH-sah
Mzee	mm-ZAY
Sabaki (River)	sah-BAH-kee
Swahili	swah-HEE-lee

This book has been adapted from the original e-book *Owen and Mzee,* by coauthors Isabella Hatkoff, Craig Hatkoff, and Dr. Paula Kahumbu, which was first launched on the WNBC New York Five O'Clock News, April 29, 2005, as part of the Tribeca Film Festival.

Library of Congress Cataloging-in-Publication Data
Hatkoff, Isabella.
Owen and Mzee : the true story of a remarkable friendship / told by Isabella Hatkoff, Craig Hatkoff, and Paula Kahumbu; photographs by Peter Greste.—1st ed.   p. cm.
"This book has been adapted from the original e-book, *Owen and Mzee*, which was first launched on the WNBC New York Five O'Clock News as part of the Tribeca Film Festival"—T.p. verso.
ISBN 0-439-82973-9
1. Hippopotamus—Behavior—Kenya—Juvenile literature. 2. Aldabra tortoise—Behavior—Kenya—Juvenile literature. 3. Social behavior in animals—Kenya—Juvenile literature. I. Hatkoff, Craig. II. Kahumbu, P. (Paula) III. Greste, Peter, ill. IV. Title.

QL737.U57H38 2006   599.63'5139—dc22   2005021341

10 9 8 7 6 5 4 3 2   06 07 08 09 10

Printed in Singapore 46 • First edition, March 2006
Book design by Elizabeth B. Parisi • The text was set in 14.5pt. Adobe Garamond.

We extend our heartfelt appreciation to all the everyday heroes, whose names are unknown to us, who helped to rescue Owen. We are indebted to the devoted team at Haller Park, especially Sabine Baer, Rehabilitation and Ecosystems Manager, and Dr. Zahoor Kashmiri, wildlife veterinarian. We express our special appreciation to Stephen Tuei, Chief Animal Caretaker, for his contributions to the making of this book.

We also thank Dr. Harold Koplewicz and the NYU Child Study Center, and our friends at WNBC in New York who launched this story at the 2005 Tribeca Film Festival. Special thanks go to Juliana Hatkoff, who helped us write a better book.

We particularly acknowledge Dr. Joshua Ginsberg, Vice President, Conservation Operations, Wildlife Conservation Society, based at the Bronx Zoo, New York, and faculty member at Columbia University's Department of Ecology, Evolution, and Environmental Biology, for serving as an expert consultant for this project.

Above all, we want to thank Owen and Mzee, who inspire and delight children and adults everywhere.

Dear Friends,

Like so many people everywhere, we were captivated by an incredible photograph that appeared in newspapers in January 2005. It showed a baby hippo snuggling with a giant tortoise. We read that the unlikely pair, now inseparable companions, were brought together as a result of the tsunami that occurred in the Indian Ocean on December 26, 2004. As father and daughter, we were deeply moved by their story of resilience and friendship, and we wanted to learn more.

We contacted Dr. Paula Kahumbu, General Manager of Haller Park, where Owen and Mzee now live, and Dr. Paula shared with us the whole story of Owen's dramatic rescue from the sea and the healing that Owen drew from his friendship with Mzee. We all decided to write a book together that would share Owen and Mzee's adventure with children and adults everywhere.

Then Peter Greste, the photographer whose image brought Owen and Mzee to the world's attention, happily agreed to take part. Before we knew it, this book was born.

We hope the incredible story you are about to read inspires you as much as it has us. It shows how connected we really are with everyone and everything. It is also a vivid reminder that even when the world seems its bleakest, we should never give up!

With love and hope,

Isabella   Craig Hatkoff

THIS IS THE TRUE STORY of two great friends: a baby hippopotamus named Owen and a 130-year-old giant tortoise named Mzee.

The hippo was not always friends with the tortoise. He wasn't always known as "Owen." And Owen was not always famous the world over. Here is how it all happened.

Before the baby hippopotamus became known as Owen, he lived with his mother in a group, or pod, with about twenty other hippos. They fed and wallowed in and around the Sabaki River in Kenya, a nation on the east coast of Africa. When he was about one year old, heavy December rains flooded the river. The racing water washed Owen and his family down the river, until the freshwater became salty and the river flowed into the Indian Ocean, near the small coastal town of Malindi.

For days, the people of Malindi tried to chase the hippos back up the river. But the hippos enjoyed grazing the grasses along the shore and in the villagers' yards. Since hippos are the most dangerous animals in Africa, and a full-grown adult can weigh as much as 8,000 pounds, there was little the people could do.

Owen lived in a pod of hippos, like this one.

On the morning of December 26, 2004, the sea suddenly rushed high onto the beaches, and surging waves pounded the shore. Many of the villagers' boats were damaged, and many fishermen had to be rescued. Before long, the sea was calm again, but it was a frightening time for everybody. A day passed before anyone thought to check on the hippos. The villagers now saw only one hippopotamus in the sea – a baby without his mother, stranded on a sandy coral reef among the sea grass. Tired and frightened, he was unable to reach the shore on his own.

Soon, hundreds of villagers and visitors were working together to help the young hippo. They knew that he would become sick if he stayed in the salty seawater for long. They used ropes, boats, fishing nets, and even cars to try to rescue him and bring him ashore to safety.

Malindi fishermen and their colorfully decorated wooden boats

Owen was
stranded
alone
on a reef.

It was soon clear that a rescue wouldn't be easy. Though the baby hippo was only about two feet tall, he weighed a hefty 600 pounds and was slippery and strong. And the hippo was alarmed by all the human commotion. Angrily, he broke through their nets and escaped from their ropes. Hours went by, and the anxious crowds of people who gathered to watch feared that the hippo could not be saved.

Finally, with a stronger shark net, the rescuers were able to catch the hippo. A brave visitor named Owen Sobien tackled him, stopping him long enough to let others secure the net. That is why, when it came time to choose a name for the hippo, it seemed only right that he should be called "Owen."

At last, the rescuers towed the baby hippo toward land. When they reached the shore, a loud, joyous cheer went up from the thousand men, women, boys, and girls who now crowded the beach. Their happy cries could be heard almost a mile away.

Wrapped in the net, Owen was hoisted into the back of a pickup truck and brought to a shady spot.

The cheers could be heard almost a mile away.

People weren't sure where Owen should be taken next. They called Haller Park, an animal sanctuary about fifty miles away, near the city of Mombasa. Dr. Paula Kahumbu, the manager, immediately offered Owen a place to live there. She explained that he could never be returned to the wild. Since he was still a baby, he wouldn't have learned yet how to fend for himself. And he would never be welcomed into another hippo pod – he would be seen as an intruder and attacked. But they would take good care of him in Haller Park. Dr. Paula offered to drive to Malindi herself to bring Owen to his new home.

Dr. Paula knew she would need help. She asked the chief animal caretaker, Stephen Tuei, to come along with her. She knew that Stephen had a special way with animals. Some people said he could even talk to them. Dr. Paula and Stephen quickly set off in her small truck to Malindi.

Meanwhile, ecologist Sabine Baer got to work with others at Haller Park to prepare for Owen's arrival.

Dr. Paula, Stephen, and Sabine
were eager to help the orphaned hippo.

When Dr. Paula and Stephen arrived in Malindi, they helped to remove the nets and lead Owen out of the pickup. But Owen became angrier than ever and charged at the people gathered around. They tried to help him calm down by wrapping a blanket around his head. That way, he wouldn't see the things that were upsetting him. But Owen was angry about that, too. After many hours, about a dozen rescuers managed to move Owen from the pickup into Dr. Paula's truck, tying him so that he would be safe during the long drive to Haller Park.

Everyone tried to make Owen as comfortable as possible.

Meanwhile, Sabine and other workers prepared a large enclosure for Owen. They chose a part of the park that had a pond and a mud wallow, as well as tall trees and brush – everything a hippo could want. The area was already home to a number of bushbucks, vervet monkeys, and a giant Aldabra tortoise called Mzee.

Mzee, whose name means "wise old man" in the Swahili language, was the oldest creature in the park. At about 130 years of age, he had been alive since before Stephen's great-grandmother was born. He wasn't very friendly, except to Stephen, who seemed to know just what he liked, such as getting tickled under the chin. Otherwise, Mzee kept to himself.

No one could have guessed how Mzee's life was about to change.

Stephen tickles Mzee.

Finally, Dr. Paula and Stephen arrived with Owen, who was now weak and exhausted. As soon as the ropes that held him were untied, Owen scrambled from the truck directly to Mzee, resting in a corner of the enclosure. Owen crouched behind Mzee, the way baby hippos often hide behind their mothers for protection. At first, Mzee wasn't happy about this attention. He hissed at Owen and crawled away. But Owen, who could easily keep up with the old tortoise, did not give up. Slowly, as the night went on, Mzee began to accept his new companion. When the park workers checked on them in the morning, Owen was snuggled up against Mzee. And Mzee didn't seem to mind at all.

That night, Owen and Mzee snuggled close together.

Over the next few days, Mzee continued to crawl away, and Owen continued to follow him. But sometimes it was Owen who would walk away from Mzee, and Mzee who would follow. Bit by bit, Mzee grew friendlier.

At first, Owen wouldn't eat any of the leaves left out for him. Stephen and the other caretakers were worried that he would weaken even more. Then they noticed Owen feeding right beside Mzee, as if Mzee were showing him how to eat. Or perhaps it was Mzee's protective presence that helped Owen feel calm enough to eat. No one will ever know. But it was clear that the bond between Owen and Mzee was helping the baby hippo to recover from being separated from his mother and stranded in the sea.

With Mzee by his side, Owen began to eat.

Both hippos and tortoises love the water.

As the weeks went on, Owen and Mzee spent more and more time together. Soon, they were inseparable. Their bond remains very strong to this day. They swim together, eat together, drink together, and sleep next to each other. They rub noses. Owen leads the way to different parts of the enclosure, then Mzee leads the way. Owen playfully nuzzles Mzee's neck, and Mzee stretches his neck forward asking for more, just as he does when Stephen tickles him under the chin. Though both animals could easily injure each other, they are gentle with one another. A sense of trust has grown between them.

Owen nuzzles Mzee's ticklish neck.

Wildlife experts are still puzzled about how this unlikely friendship came to be. Most have never heard of a mammal, such as Owen, and a reptile, such as Mzee, forming such a strong bond.

Perhaps for Owen, it happened this way: Young hippos like Owen need their mothers in order to survive. An old, slow tortoise like Mzee can never protect Owen the way a fierce mother hippo could. But since Mzee's coloring and rounded shape are similar to a hippo's, it's possible that to Owen, Mzee looks like the hippo mother he needs.

Harder to explain is the affection that Mzee seems to show for Owen. Like most Aldabra tortoises, Mzee had always preferred to be alone. But sometimes these tortoises live in groups, and perhaps Mzee sees Owen as a fellow tortoise, the first tortoise he is willing to spend time with. Or perhaps Mzee knows that Owen isn't a tortoise, but likes him anyway.

The reasons are unclear. But science can't always explain what the heart already knows: Our most important friends are sometimes those we least expected.

Mzee and Owen play "follow-the-leader."

News of Owen and Mzee's friendship quickly spread around the world. People all over have come to love Owen, who endured so much, yet never gave up, and Mzee, who became Owen's friend when he needed one most. Their photographs have appeared in countless newspaper and magazine articles. Television programs and even a film documentary have been made about them. Visitors come to Haller Park every day to meet the famous friends.

Owen and Mzee look out for each other.

Owen suffered a great loss. But with the help of many caring people, and through his own extraordinary resilience, Owen has begun a new, happy life. Most remarkable is the role that Mzee has played. We'll never know for sure whether Owen sees Mzee as a mother, a father, or a very good friend. But it really doesn't matter. What matters is that Owen isn't alone – and neither is Mzee.

And that is the true story of Owen and Mzee, two great friends.

Owen's future is bright.

MORE ABOUT...

KENYA

The country of Kenya sits on the equator on the eastern coast of Africa. Most Kenyans speak Swahili, as well as their own traditional language. Mzee [mm-ZAY] is a Swahili word meaning "elder," or "wise old man."

MALINDI

Malindi is a small town on the coast of the Indian Ocean. Many residents are fishermen. Malindi is known for its beautiful beaches and coral reefs, and thousands of visitors stay in its hotels. Many visitors took part in Owen's rescue. The small coastal city of Mombasa is about fifty miles south of Malindi.

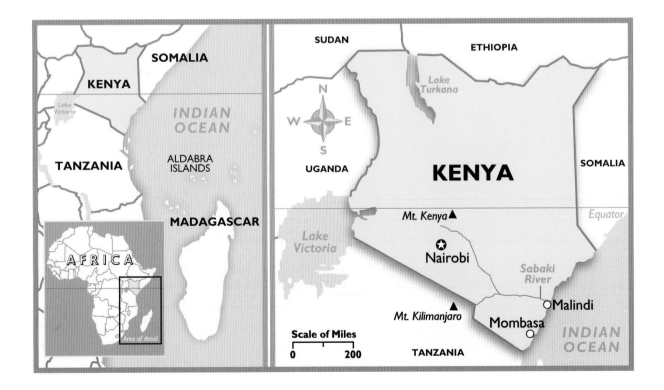

HIPPOPOTAMI

Hippos live in and around rivers and lakes of sub-Saharan Africa. Their name comes from the Latin words for "horse" (*hippo*) and "river" (*potamus*) – a "river horse." Babies are dependent on their mothers for up to four years. Hippos are easily annoyed and extremely aggressive. They use their speed, size, and powerful jaws to protect their territory from intruders. But they do not attack for food: They eat only grasses. They live up to forty years in the wild and sixty years in captivity.

ALDABRA TORTOISES

The Aldabra [al-DAH-brah] tortoise, found on the Aldabra Islands in the Indian Ocean, is the largest species of tortoise in the world. They are similar to the better-known Galapagos tortoise. As adults, they grow to as much as four feet in length, and live up to 200 years. Mzee's caretakers guess that he is about 130 years old. Mzee, like many Aldabra tortoises, was probably taken from his home by sailors for food. He may have reached Africa by escaping the ship, perhaps during a shipwreck.

OWEN AND MZEE AND THE TSUNAMI OF DECEMBER 2004

Owen was found stranded the day after the devastating tsunami [su-NAH-mee] that occurred in the eastern Indian Ocean on December 26, 2004. The towering waves of the tsunami were caused by a massive earthquake under the ocean floor near Indonesia. More than 175,000 people lost their lives, and entire towns were destroyed. By the time the tsunami traveled 4,000 miles to the shores of Kenya, the waves had lost much of their force and damage there was less severe. But the whole world was shocked and saddened at the news of this disaster. The story of Owen's rescue and friendship with Mzee filled people everywhere with hope. It reminded us all that even though terrible, unexpected things happen, the power of courage, love, and the preciousness of life will prevail.

THE FUTURE FOR OWEN AND MZEE

The caretakers plan to keep Owen and Mzee together as long as they both wish to be together. When Owen seemed ready for the company of other hippos, he was moved to a larger pond where the park's other hippos live, including a lonely female named Cleo. Mzee was moved along with him, and they are still close companions.

HALLER PARK

This animal sanctuary outside of Mombasa was created by the Lafarge Group as an ecologically sensitive way to reuse one of their old limestone quarries. More than 150 large animals live on 150 acres of a carefully planned, balanced ecosystem. Visitors are welcome every day of the week, and thousands have come especially to meet Owen and Mzee. Visit Haller Park on the Internet at www.lafargeecosystems.com for the most up-to-date information on Owen and Mzee.

A DISCUSSION GUIDE for this book, *Cultivating Resiliency: A Guide for Parents and School Personnel*, has been prepared by psychologists at the NYU Child Study Center. Visit www.scholastic.com/discussionguides to download a free copy.

Stephen Tuei checks on Owen and Mzee.

PICTURE CREDITS